NEW VANGUARD 326

SOVIET CRUISERS

From the October Revolution to World
War II

ALEXANDER HILL   ILLUSTRATED BY PAUL WRIGHT

OSPREY PUBLISHING

Bloomsbury Publishing Plc

Kemp House, Chawley Park, Cumnor Hill, Oxford OX2 9PH, UK

29 Earlsfort Terrace, Dublin 2, Ireland

1385 Broadway, 5th Floor, New York, NY 10018, USA

E-mail: info@ospreypublishing.com

www.ospreypublishing.com

OSPREY is a trademark of Osprey Publishing Ltd

First published in Great Britain in 2024

A catalogue record for this book is available from the British Library.

ISBN: PB 9781472859334; eBook 9781472859327

ePDF 9781472859358; XML 9781472859341

24 25 26 27 28 10 9 8 7 6 5 4 3 2 1

Index by Richard Munro
Typeset by PDQ Digital Media Solutions, Bungay, UK
Printed and bound in India by Replika Press Private Ltd.

FSC
www.fsc.org

MIX
Paper from
responsible sources
FSC® C016779

Osprey Publishing supports the Woodland Trust, the UK's leading woodland conservation charity.

To find out more about our authors and books visit **www.ospreypublishing.com**. Here you will find extracts, author interviews, details of forthcoming events and the option to sign up for our newsletter.

Title page image: please see caption on page 11.

Author's Note

A note on transliteration: I have kept " and ' to represent hard and soft signs respectively when providing words originating in Cyrillic in English transliteration.

CONTENTS

SOVIET CRUISERS

From the October Revolution to World War II

INTRODUCTION

During the period between World War I and World War II, the role of the cruiser in naval warfare was typically seen as primarily involving the attack and defence of maritime communications on the high seas, as well as scouting for a fleet in the vast expanses of the world's oceans. Built with much more of an emphasis on speed rather than armoured protection, cruisers could in principle successfully engage most vessels they might encounter with similar speeds, such as other cruisers and destroyers, and outrun most larger vessels with heavier firepower and much better armoured protection, such as battleships. Although the battlecruiser and 'pocket' battleship challenged this schema – and cruisers would be divided into heavy and light types – this basic conception survived into the early phases of World War II.

In principle, this traditional view of the place of the cruiser in a navy was shared by many Soviet naval officers and theorists during the first decades of the existence of the Soviet Navy. However, not all Soviet naval theorists of the interwar period saw the same need for cruisers in a navy they thought might be better focused on coastal defence and reliant on larger numbers of smaller vessels than fewer larger vessels such as cruisers and battleships. Proponents of *Jeune École* (Young School) ideas in the Soviet Navy still often saw a significant role for cruisers in attacking enemy lines of communications – and as focal points for lighter forces – but *Jeune École* ideas tended not to see a role for larger, heavy cruisers. However, the voices of those orientated towards such *Jeune École* ideas in Soviet naval circles were increasingly

The Bogatir'-class cruiser *Oleg*, shown here in 1906. Note the revised bridge structure compared to the arrangement as constructed and depicted in Plate A (*see* page 9), and with which it fought at Tsushima in 1905. (Macpherson)

silenced as the 1930s progressed by proponents of the idea that the Soviet Union should have an 'ocean-going' fleet – an idea driven by Soviet leader Joseph Stalin's ambitions for the Soviet Union to be seen as a great power. However, Soviet political and military leaders were still left facing issues with the capabilities of Soviet industry. Ambitious pre-war plans for heavy cruisers would ultimately remain unrealized given many other competing claims for resources.

As Stalin's rapid industrialisation of the 1930s got underway, Soviet shipbuilding capacity nonetheless increased. In addition to retaining the surviving pre-Soviet cruisers *Aurora* and *Komintern*, the Soviet Navy would in the late 1920s receive the completed cruisers *Profintern* (later *Krasnii Krim*), *Chervona Ukraina* and *Krasnii Kavkaz*, inherited in a partly constructed state from the Tsarist regime, before going on to receive units of the wholly Soviet-constructed Project 26 and 26-bis in the latter part of the 1930s. A number of vessels of a successor Chapaev class (Project 68) were laid down at the end of the 1930s, but none were completed during the war. However, plans for heavier cruisers had to be shelved in the face of competing claims on resources, and even after World War II, Stalin's Soviet Union would continue to build essentially light gun-armed cruisers. Only after Stalin's death would such cruisers finally fall out of favour in the Soviet Union.

When World War II broke out in Europe in September 1939, the Soviet Union did not have any of its existing cruisers in its Northern and Pacific Fleets – the two fleets with ready access to the high seas – and instead had them all concentrated in the larger Baltic and Black Sea Fleets. Lacking ready access to the high seas, Soviet cruisers bottled up in the Baltic and Black Seas were not typically in a position to carry out the sort of roles for which cruisers were usually intended, and indeed which seemed to be being fulfilled by many British cruisers – such as those that engaged the German pocket battleship *Graf Spee* off Montevideo in late 1939, for example.

In the European theatre, major powers soon realized that the 'traditional' schema for the use of cruisers was not going to be compatible with the developing operational requirements of World War II, where even those British cruisers initially being used as intended quickly ran out of German targets. It did not take long for a cruiser to be seen as a heavier 'maid of all work', like their smaller brethren the destroyers, and in no fleet was this more obviously the case than the Soviet one. In some senses, *Jeune École* ideas won through in the end through force of circumstances rather than intent.

From conducting shore bombardment to carrying men and materiel into besieged ports, the Soviet cruisers of the Black Sea Fleet saw very active wartime service – with the Black Sea Fleet losing the sole Soviet cruiser lost outright during the war. In the Baltic Sea, the cruisers spent much of the war bottled up in the Leningrad region, although the first months of the war saw considerable activity without the irrecoverable loss of a cruiser.

This book examines the construction and operational use of the Soviet cruiser force from the time of the October Revolution of 1917 that brought the Bolsheviks to power in Russia through to the end of World War II. Particular attention is paid to their operational use.

Although no longer serving as a cruiser but as a depot ship, the aged armoured cruiser *Pamiat' Azova* was also sunk in Soviet service by a British MTB, in its case during a daring British attack on the harbour at Kronstadt in August 1919. (NH, 88746)

CRUISERS LAID DOWN DURING THE TSARIST PERIOD

The Soviet cruiser force in the Revolution and Civil War, 1917–21

When the Bolshevik Party seized power in Russia in the name of the Soviet movement in October 1917, the new Soviet government inherited a sizeable cruiser force from the Tsarist and Provisional Governments (the latter in power from March–October 1917). By the time of the Bolshevik Revolution in October 1917, the navy was called the Fleet of the Russian Democratic Republic, as it had been named on 3 September 1917 under the Provisional Government. On 11 February 1918, the Bolsheviks renamed the fleet the Workers' and Peasants' Red Fleet.

For much of the Russian Civil War – largely over by early 1921 – the Bolsheviks did not control most of the coastline of the former Tsarist empire, and hence former Tsarist naval power based on the Black Sea, in the far north or in the Far East. It was in these regions that foreign forces intervening in the Civil War – and in particular those of Britain and France – were by virtue of their naval power able to land forces and dominate such coastal areas. Consequently, only the Baltic region would see meaningful Soviet naval activity during the Civil War period.

The Soviet government had made peace with Germany with the Brest-Litovsk treaty of 3 March 1918. After this peace, even in the Baltic close to the Russian capital Petrograd, the Soviet fleet could no longer maintain a presence in many nearby non-Russian parts of the Russian Empire that were either now under German control or about to receive their independence. New governments such as that in Finland were extremely hostile to the Bolsheviks. As a result of these circumstances, the so-called 'Ice Expedition' of March 1918 saw five Soviet cruisers – out of a total of 226 Soviet vessels – make their way from Helsingfors in Finland to Petrograd in tense circumstances. On 12 March 1918, the cruisers *Riurik*, *Admiral Makarov* and *Bogatir'* left Helsingfors, along with the battleships *Petropavlovsk*, *Gangut*, *Sevastopol'* and *Poltava*, accompanied by the icebreakers *Ermak* and *Volinets*. However, the passage of subsequent vessels was made more difficult by the fact that the *Volinets* would subsequently go over to the Finnish Whites (serving as *Wäinämöinen*

The sole Soviet cruiser in the far north after the Revolution of 1917, the protected cruiser *Askol'd* was captured by the British in 1918 and renamed *Glory IV*. It is shown here as such in 1919. (Getty)

with the Finns before becoming *Suur Tõll* in Estonia – where it remains as a museum ship), leaving the Bolsheviks with only *Ermak* to give them significant icebreaking capability. Only on 5 April 1918 could the cruisers *Baian* and *Oleg* make the passage to Kronstadt, assisted initially only by port icebreakers. This episode in Soviet naval history is seen in the Russian and Soviet literature as one of the earliest 'achievements' of the Soviet naval forces.

It was at Kronstadt, near Petrograd, that most of the Soviet Baltic cruiser force languished in port for the period of the Civil War – and where many of their crew members were either fighting on land or had abandoned their posts and simply gone home.

Tables 1–3 list cruisers that at some point were at least in the nominal service of Soviet forces during the period of the Revolution and Civil War in Russia from 1917–21, divided up by fleet and flotilla.

Table 1: Cruisers in Soviet service 1917–21 – Baltic Fleet (Naval Forces of the Baltic Sea)

Name	Class	Laid down/ launched/ completed	Displacement (tonnes)	Main armament (in 1917)	Max speed (knots)	Fate (to 1927)
Aurora	Pallada	1897/1900/1903	6,731	14x152mm	20	In service (Baltic)
Admiral Makarov	Baian	1905/1906/1908 (France)	7,835	3x203mm	21	Sold to Germany for scrap (1922)
Baian	Baian	1905/1907/1911	7,835	3x203mm	21	8x152mm guns removed (1918), scrapped (1922)
Bogatir'	Bogatir'	1899/1901/1902 (Germany)	7,428	16x130mm	23	Scrapped (1922), parts used for repair of *Komintern* (see Black Sea Fleet)
Diana	Pallada	1897/1899/1901	6,731	10x130mm	20	Mothballed (1918) – part of armament removed, scrapped (1922)
Gromovoi		1898/1899/1900	12,359	6x203mm	20.1	Mothballed (1918) – part of armament removed (1919), sold to Germany for scrap (1922)
Oleg	Bogatir'	1902/1903/1904	6,975	16x130mm	23	Sunk by British MTBs (June 1919), part of armament removed (1919), raised and scrapped (1938)
Riurik		1905/1906/1908 (UK)	16,930	8x203mm	21	Broken up (1923) – main armament to a fort near Leningrad
Rossiia		1895/1896/1897	12,195	6x203mm	19	Mothballed (1918), part of armament removed (1919), sold to Germany for scrap (1922)

Table 2: Cruisers in Soviet service 1917–21 – Black Sea Fleet (Naval Forces of the Black Sea)

Name	Class	Laid down/ launched/ completed	Displacement (tonnes)	Main armament (in 1917)	Max speed (knots)	Fate (to 1927)
Kagul (to 1907 *Ochakov*)	Bogatir'	1901/1902/1905	7,070	14x130mm	23	Captured by German forces (1918), transferred to Whites (1918) and evacuated to Constantinople (as *General Kornilov*) (1920) before being interned in France (1920)
Pamiat' Merkuriia	Bogatir'	1901/1902/1905	7,070	16x152mm	23	Captured by German forces, transferred to Whites and then Anglo-French forces (1918); abandoned in disabled state by White forces (1920); repaired and re-entered service with Soviet naval forces as *Komintern* (from December 1922)
Prut		1902–05 (in USA for Turkey as *Medjidieh*)	4,090	10x130mm (as rearmed by Russia)	22	Struck a mine off Odessa and sunk, before being raised and entering Russian service (1915); captured by German forces from Soviets and returned to Turkey (1918); remained in Turkish service

Table 3: Cruisers in Soviet service 1917–21 – Flotilla of the Arctic Ocean (Naval Forces of the North Sea)

Name	Class	Laid down/ launched/ completed	Displacement (tonnes)	Main armament (in 1917)	Max speed (knots)	Fate (to 1927)
Askol'd		1899/1900/1902 (Germany)	5,905	12x152mm	23	Briefly interned by China (1904); Siberian Flotilla then Arctic Ocean Flotilla (1905–16); captured by British from Soviets (1918); returned from UK to Soviet government and scrapped in Germany (1922)

Although few Soviet naval vessels saw action even in the Baltic, an exception to this rule was the protected cruiser *Oleg*, that saw significant activity in the Baltic before being sunk by British forces in June 1919. *Oleg*'s basic characteristics as completed are provided in Table 4.

Table 4: *Oleg* – specifications (as constructed)		
Displacement	Normal (tonnes)	7,400
	Full (tonnes)	8,000
Dimensions	Maximum length (m)	134.1
	Maximum width (m)	16.6
Draught (as designed) (m)		6.3
Speed (maximum)	Design (kts)	23
	Actual (kts)	20.6
Range (at 10kts)	Design (miles)	5,000
	Actual (miles)	2,400
Armament*	Main	12x152mm (45 cal)
	Secondary	12x75mm (50 cal), 8x47mm (43.5 cal)
	Torpedoes	2x381mm (submerged)
Armoured protection	deck (maximum horizontal)/bridge (maximum)/ casemates (maximum), turrets (maximum)	35/140/80/125
Crew		582

*For naval landings, the ship was provided with 2x37mm guns.

The *Oleg* is shown in Plate A as it fought at the naval battle of Tsushima against the Japanese in 1905, and in a post-Tsushima configuration with revised bridge structure in the first photograph in this book. By the time it was in Bolshevik hands, its main armament consisted of 130mm 55-calibre Obr 1913 guns – a superior weapon to the original 152mm armament of most Russian cruisers inherited by the Bolsheviks both prior to and after the October 1917 Revolution.

At the end of November 1918, in Bolshevik service – and shortly before the arrival of British forces in the region – the cruiser *Oleg* and destroyer *Metkii* had escorted three transports into Estonian waters, where the transports landed troops who would assist in the capture of Narva by the Soviet 7th Army. During December 1918, *Oleg* would again be at sea off Revel (later Tallinn), during which time, after having engaged in limited shore bombardment, it was hunted by British naval forces but was able to return to base. As White troops under the command of General Iudenich pressed on towards Petrograd from the Baltic region during the summer of 1919

OLEG (BOGATIR' CLASS) IN 1904–05

The Bolshevik government inherited a number of cruisers of the Bogatir' class in 1917, with one of them, *Pamiat Merkuriia*, going on to serve with the Soviet Navy in the Black Sea during the Great Patriotic War of 1941–45 as the *Komintern*. A second vessel of the class to see active service with the Bolsheviks was the *Oleg*. This vessel would see active service during the initial period of Civil War and foreign intervention immediately after the October 1917 Revolution, until sunk in the Gulf of Finland by a torpedo from a British motor torpedo boat on 18 June 1919.

Distinctive of cruisers of the class are the large twin turrets fore and aft as well as ram bow and detail relating to their anchoring system. The *Oleg* is pictured here in a paint scheme worn by Russian vessels that saw action in the Far East during the Russo–Japanese War of 1904–05. The iconic cruiser *Aurora* wore the same scheme against the Japanese (*see* Plate B). At this time, the *Oleg* had only recently been completed, and was armed with its initial armament of 12 152mm (45 cal) guns – two in each of the two turrets fore and aft with a further four in casemates. The remaining four 152mm guns were interspersed with six of its 75mm (50 cal) on the port and starboard sides.

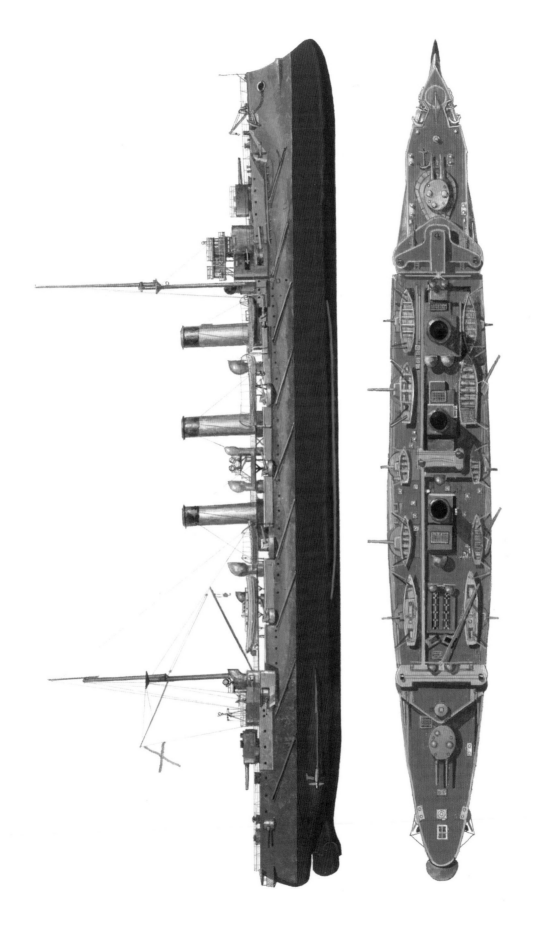

– supported by British naval forces – *Oleg* was again in action bombarding coastal forts that had rebelled against the Bolsheviks and that would soon be captured by Bolshevik-led forces with its support. It was shortly after performing in this role that an attack by British MTBs near Kronstadt saw the *Oleg* struck by what is widely suggested to have been a single torpedo shortly after midnight on 18 June 1919. Within 12 minutes it had sunk in shallow waters, five of its crew perishing. It is worth noting here that during an attack on the naval base at Kronstadt in August that year, British MTBs were also able to sink the 6,734-tonne *Pamiat' Azova* (previously *Dvina*) – a vessel that was built as an armoured cruiser (6,674 tonnes – laid down in 1886, launched in 1888 and entered service in 1890) but was serving as a depot ship when it was sunk (see NVG 305).

After the October 1917 Revolution, many nominally Soviet cruisers in the Black Sea passed through the hands of German forces, the Ukrainian Rada and the British and French or White forces. Here, the Bogatir'-class protected cruiser *Kagul* – later renamed *General Kornilov* by the Whites – is shown at Batumi in March 1916. (Alamy)

The battleship *Sevastopol'* leads the cruiser *Admiral Makarov* through the ice on their passage to Kronstandt from Helsingfors in March 1918. The evacuation of these and other naval vessels from former Russian imperial possessions was seen as a significant achievement by Bolshevik naval forces. (Fine Art Images/ Heritage-Images/TopFoto)

As is apparent from the tables provided on the Soviet cruiser force during the Civil War period and immediately after, very few of the cruisers inherited by the new Soviet government from the Provisional and Tsarist regimes remained in Soviet service far into the 1920s. Having in the main languished in port in increasingly poor states of repair as the Civil War progressed, most ships were not deemed worth rehabilitating in the harsh financial circumstances in which the new Soviet government found itself in the early 1920s. Not only the navy but also the army suffered severe cutbacks that would see the Soviet Union completely abandon having naval forces either in the far north or Far East of the USSR (leaving what would become the NKVD to police its maritime borders in those regions). Hence, by 1927, of the cruisers inherited from the Tsarist regime, only *Aurora* and *Komintern* remained in service with Soviet naval forces, although by this point completion of the hulls of three Svetlana-class vessels that had been partially completed under Tsarist rule was underway. These three light cruisers would, together with *Aurora* and *Komintern*, give the Soviet Navy of the World War II period a total of six cruiser-sized vessels with significant Tsarist heritage, the sixth being the minelayer *Marti*, based on the former Tsarist royal yacht. The design, construction, modification and operational service of these six vessels will be the focus of much of this book before looking at those cruisers that served with the Soviet Navy that were wholly constructed after the Revolution of October 1917.

Aurora

The first of the cruisers of the Soviet Navy – serving for the entire period with which this book is concerned – is undoubtedly the most famous, having played a headline role in the Bolshevik seizure of power in October 1917.

A veteran of the Russo-Japanese War (see NVG 275) even before its starring role in the October Revolution, *Aurora* remains afloat today as a museum ship in what is now St Petersburg.

The *Aurora* was conceived and designed as what for the time was a very conventional role for a cruiser – a commerce raider. A circular from the Russian Maritime Ministry of 2 March 1894 announced a competition for a new cruiser design for the Russian Navy that would ultimately result by 1896 in plans for three cruisers – *Diana*, *Pallada* and *Aurora*. All three ships were nominally laid down on 23 May 1897, although at this point their construction was well underway. On 11 May 1900, *Aurora* was launched, and by October its construction had reached the point that *Aurora* could first raise steam. *Aurora* would first venture from Kronstadt only on 28 July 1902, and would be subject to lengthy trials and modification such that it would only finally enter service in late 1903.

The Pallada-class protected cruiser *Aurora* had an active career before coming under Bolshevik control in 1917. Here, it is shown while still in Tsarist service in 1916. (Getty)

Aurora was very much a conventional cruiser design for the period, with those developing it paying close attention to foreign designs, particularly those of Germany and Britain. Its main armoured belt had horizontal armour with a maximum 38mm thickness (with an armoured bridge with a maximum 152mm armour and 89mm armour for the main ammunition elevators) and its main armament consisted of eight 45-calibre 152mm guns. *Aurora* proved capable of making 19.2 knots, just under the design speed of 20 knots. Its basic characteristics as constructed are provided in Table 5.

Table 5: *Aurora* – specifications (as constructed)		
Displacement	Normal (tonnes)	6,731
	Full (tonnes)	7,130
Dimensions	Maximum length (m)	126.8
	Maximum width (m)	16.76
Draught (as designed) (m)		6.4
Speed (maximum)	Design (kts)	20
	Actual (kts)	19.2
Range (at 10kts)	Design (miles)	4,000
	Actual (miles)	3,300
Armament*	Main	8x152mm (45 cal)
	Secondary	24x75mm (50 cal), 4x37mm (37 cal)
	Torpedoes	3x381mm
Armoured protection	deck (maximum horizontal)/ bridge (maximum)	38mm/152mm
Crew		578

*In the event of a naval landing, *Aurora* was also provided with 2x63.5mm guns that could be mounted on either side of the officer's mess. The cruiser could also carry 35 mines.

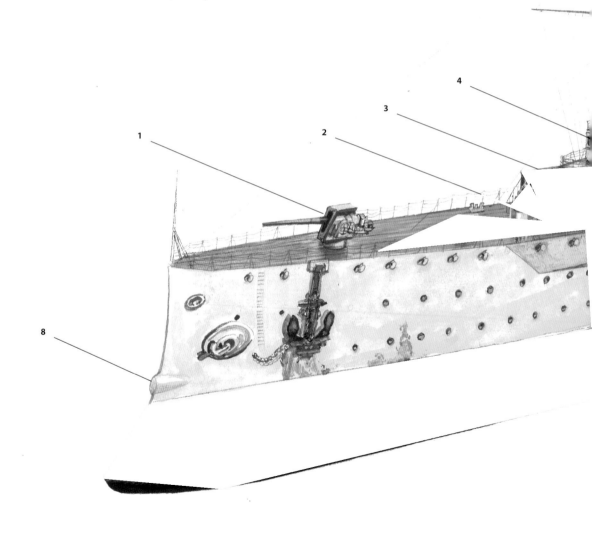

5

6

7

AURORA (PALLADA CLASS) IN 1917

The Pallada-class cruiser *Aurora* is probably one of the most famous warships of the 20th century thanks to its significant role in the October Revolution of 1917 and subsequent preservation and immortalization. It is pictured in the cutaway as it was prior to October 1917 – and in the configuration in which it appears in the battlescene in Plate C (*see* page 17). In theory, it is currently preserved in its 1917 state, although clearly Soviet engineers, academics and others involved in the restoration in the late 1980s took certain liberties during the reconstruction. While *Aurora* was due to have been equipped with six 76.2mm (30.5 cal) Lender AA guns during its refit in the winter of 1916–17, it is quite probable that none of these weapons had actually been installed by the time of the October Revolution, given that such new weapons were in short supply and that a second-class cruiser like *Aurora* would not have been a priority for them. Definitive confirmation of *Aurora*'s 1917 armament is hampered by the absence of a meaningful number of photographs of it during the revolutionary period. The current museum ship is armed with both Lender and later 45mm (46 cal) 21-K guns for saluting.

With a service history that would run through to after World War II, there was plenty of time and need for modifications to its armament. The state of *Aurora*'s armament in both 1917 and on the eve of the Great Patriotic War (the Soviet name for World War II from the time of Germany's invasion in June 1941) is indicated in Table 6.

Table 6: Armament for *Aurora*, 1917 and early 1941

Year	Armament
1917	14x152mm (45 cal) guns with 25.4mm gun shields (2 Barr and Stroud rangefinders added since initial construction)[1]
Early 1941	9 or 10x130mm Obr 1913 (55 cal) – with possibly 1x130mm B-13 (50 cal) in place of 1x130mm Obr 1913 – 2x76mm 34-K (55 cal), 2x76.2mm (30.5 cal) Lender, 3x45mm (46 cal) 21-K, plus machine guns

Operational history in Tsarist service

Aurora had an active career in Tsarist hands even before it entered Bolshevik service and ultimately became a permanent memorial to and symbol of the Bolshevik Revolution. On 2 October 1904, *Aurora* and the Russian 2nd Far Eastern Squadron set sail from Libau (Liepāja) for the Far East to face Japanese forces. During the so-called 'Hull incident' of the night of 8/9 October, the Russian squadron was assumed to be about to come under attack from destroyers – quite possibly, it was believed, of Britain's Japanese ally, but actually the vessels were British trawlers from the port of Hull – as it passed through the North Sea and on to the English Channel. *Aurora* suffered damage and casualties from 'friendly' fire from those Russian warships accompanying it.

When the Russian squadron finally reached the Far East, it suffered the ignominy of defeat at the battle of Tsushima (see CAM 330). Having arrived off Korea during the night of 14 May 1905 – the anniversary of the

1   There is discussion in the sources as to whether *Aurora* had by 1917 received any of the six 76.2mm (30.5 cal) Lender AA guns intended (and for which *Aurora* was prepped to receive) after its 1916–17 refit. I have opted to go with Aleksei Skvortsov's suggestion that it had not and that those gun positions were in fact empty at the time of the October Revolution.

After having come under Bolshevik control in 1917, many of *Aurora*'s sailors would play an active role in revolutionary events on land. Here, some of *Aurora*'s crew are shown in the Russian capital Petrograd in 1917. (Getty)

Russian Tsar Nicholas II's coronation – the squadron was subsequently all but wiped out by a Japanese force that showed far superior combat capabilities. Although the *Aurora* escaped the debacle – along with *Oleg*, depicted earlier in this book – it had suffered 18 direct hits from rounds of varying calibres that knocked out some of the ship's secondary armament and seriously damaged one of its main guns. *Aurora* itself had fired 303 152mm, 1,282 75mm and 320 37mm rounds. After a brief period of internment at

Aurora is shown here in what is probably the spring of 1918 – essentially as it was back in October 1917. (Getty)

Manila from the evening of 21 May to 15 October 1905, *Aurora* was able to make the long journey back to European Russia after the signing of the Treaty of Portsmouth brought an end to the Russo-Japanese War.

   Aurora began World War I as part of the 2nd Cruiser Brigade of the Baltic Fleet, its wartime service being relatively uneventful before it went to Kronstadt for an overhaul in September 1916. It remained undergoing its overhaul – that was supposed to include the addition of anti-aircraft armament – until making its way to Petrograd to be a participant in revolutionary events taking place in the Russian capital in 1917.

The October Revolution and Civil War

In late February 1917, the crew of the *Aurora* rebelled against the Tsarist government and the ship's officers, killing the captain, wounding the senior officer – who would later die of his wounds – and arresting many of the others. A new captain was chosen from amongst those officers supporting the revolutionary activity, although command to all intents and purposes lay with the crew. Even before October 1917, the vessel was being run by those tied to the Bolshevik Party – with a detachment of its crew having defended the Winter Palace at the time of the attempt by General Kornilov to seize power in the capital from the Provisional Government in August 1917.

   On 24 October 1917, on the eve of the October Revolution, the *Aurora* was at anchor off the Nikolaev Bridge over the Neva River in the centre of Petrograd. The next day, it was visited by a leading member of the Petrograd Military Revolutionary Committee, who instructed the crew to fire two blanks from their main armament in response to a signal from the Petropavlovsk Fortress – the signal for the storming of the seat of the Provisional Government in the Winter Palace by forces loyal to the Bolshevik-controlled Petrograd Soviet. Some of *Aurora*'s crew were themselves waiting for the signal to storm the palace, while others were engaged in the maintenance of order elsewhere in the city. At 2140hrs on 25 October, the

Resurrected by the Bolsheviks after the Civil War, the cruiser *Aurora* would have a relatively active period during the 1920s as a training vessel. Here, it is shown on a visit to the Norwegian port of Bergen in the summer of 1925. (NH, 60721)

Other than perhaps Vladimir Lenin himself, the cruiser *Aurora* probably became the most prominent symbol of the October 1917 Revolution in the Soviet Union. The ship would regularly appear on Soviet postcards commemorating the event, such as those shown here. The most typical text accompanying *Aurora* on such postcards – as in four of the cases here – was 'Glory to the Great October [Revolution]!'. (AC)

Aurora apparently fired a single blank round (rather than the two previously intended) from its fo'c'sle 152mm gun as a signal to the Bolshevik forces to attack the palace.

In the aftermath of the Bolshevik seizure of power, many of *Aurora*'s crew participated in the defence of Petrograd from the threat of White counter-revolution in the form of operations by General Krasnov. During this period of the Bolshevik taking and consolidation of power in the capital, members of the ship's crew guarded the Petropavlovsk Fortress in the centre of Petrograd, opposite the Winter Palace, and the Bolshevik headquarters at the Smol'nii Institute elsewhere in the city. *Aurora* itself was moored on the Neva.

As Russia slid deeper into civil war, although in principle the new Bolshevik leadership liked the idea of *Aurora* remaining a combat-capable warship, in the aftermath of the Brest-Litovsk peace treaty with Germany in March 1918 many sailors were either fighting elsewhere or had abandoned their posts. In these conditions – compounded by fuel and other shortages

C

AURORA (PALLADA CLASS), 25 OCTOBER 1917

On 24 October 1917, on the eve of the October Revolution, the *Aurora* was at anchor off the Nikolaev Bridge over the Neva River in the centre of Petrograd. The next day, it was instructed by a leading member of the Petrograd Military Revolutionary Committee to fire two blanks from its main armament in response to a signal from the Petropavlovsk Fortress – a signal for the storming of the seat of the Provisional Government in the Winter Palace by forces loyal to the Bolshevik-controlled Petrograd Soviet. While some of *Aurora*'s crew were themselves waiting for the signal to storm the palace, others were engaged in the maintenance of order elsewhere in the city – leaving relatively few on the ship itself. At 2140hrs on 25 October, the *Aurora* apparently fired a single blank round (rather than the two intended) from its fo'c'sle 152mm gun, signalling the revolutionary forces to storm the palace. While some authors have questioned whether the vessel even fired a single blank round, in the folklore of the Revolution it did so – spawning many Soviet works of art of that dramatic moment. This illustration shows a version of that scene.

– the Bolshevik leadership decided to keep as active only a small proportion of the vessels nominally under their control capable of combat operations, with the remainder – including *Aurora* – being mothballed. On 29 July 1918, *Aurora* was transferred into a state of long-term preservation without having fully completed its overhaul of 1916–17.

Soviet service from 1922 onwards

Aurora would only emerge from its state of preservation on 30 October 1922 before being ready after refit and repairs to raise the naval ensign again on 23 February 1923. Its days in front-line service were now ostensibly over, for it was to serve as a training ship. Although only a training ship, at this time the Soviet Navy had few large warships other than the few surviving Tsarist-era battleships kept in service with which to show the Soviet flag abroad. Indeed, as has already been noted, of the pre-revolutionary Soviet cruisers, only *Aurora* and *Komintern* would serve the new Soviet government into the mid-1920s. *Aurora* was involved in showing the Soviet flag abroad during the 1920s in a series of visits to Scandinavia and Germany (during the time before the rise of Adolf Hitler, when relations between the Soviet Union and Germany were cordial), but otherwise had a relatively quiet life as a training ship. By early 1933, the vessel was in need again of an overhaul, but with Soviet shipyards busy with new construction its overhaul was delayed and then called off, and in 1935 it became a static training 'barge'. Indeed, shortly before the outbreak of the Great Patriotic War in June 1941, the decision was taken to give another vessel its name, but war would stop this from happening.

At the outbreak of the Great Patriotic War, *Aurora* was moored at Oranienbaum to the south-west of what was now the city of Leningrad (the former Petrograd). As German forces advanced on the city, the *Aurora* was gradually stripped of much of its crew and armament. Bombed and shelled by German forces, by winter an absence of heat and light on the ship left it with only a nominal crew responsible for its flag and single functioning 76mm anti-aircraft gun. Only with the lifting of the blockade of Leningrad in early 1944 was *Aurora* safe from German shelling.

It was during the summer of 1944 that the decision was taken for *Aurora* to become in part a museum ship and in part a training vessel to be moored near the Nakhimov naval academy in Leningrad. Ultimately losing its training function, *Aurora* has since then served as a floating museum at various moorings in Leningrad – now St Petersburg. During the 1980s, it underwent a major overhaul and refit that would see the ship returned to an approximation of its state in October 1917.

Many generations of Soviet and Russian sailors, tourists and newlyweds have had their picture taken with *Aurora* seemingly timeless in the background. Thanks in part to its immortalization in Soviet propaganda relating to the Revolution, it remains one of the most iconic warships afloat.

Komintern (previously *Pamiat' Merkuriia, Kagul*)

Another cruiser constructed by the Tsarist government that would see service in the Soviet Navy from the period of the October 1917 Revolution through to the Great Patriotic War was the *Komintern*, which started its life as *Kagul* but was renamed *Pamiat' Merkuriia* shortly after entering service in 1907. It was a member of the Bogatir' class of protected cruisers constructed to

act as scouts for the Russian Fleet – a member of the same class as *Oleg* covered earlier in this book. Although the lead ship of the class, *Bogatir'*, was constructed in Germany, *Kagul* was built in Nikolaev on the Black Sea. Its lengthy construction period saw it laid down on 23 August 1901, launched on 20 May 1903, but not actually entering service until 31 January 1907 – around which time it became *Pamiat' Merkuriia* (19 April 1907). Confusingly, another vessel of the class then became *Kagul*. Its renaming continued as it was briefly *Getman (Hetman) Ivan Mazepa* from October–December 1918 before reverting to being *Pamiat' Merkuriia* – only finally becoming *Komintern* on 31 December 1922.

As a member of the same class of ship as *Oleg*, *Pamiat' Merkuriia*'s basic characteristics as it entered service were very similar to those of its sister vessel and need not be repeated here. Given the lengthy period with which *Pamiat' Merkuriia/Komintern* served with the Russian and Soviet navies, there was plenty of time for modifications to be made to its armament. Perhaps the most striking change was the removal of the twin turrets fore and aft – replaced with single 130mm (55 cal) Obr 1913 mounts at the beginning of the 1930s. The removal of one of its three funnels prior to the Great Patriotic War also represented a major change to the ship's profile.

There is considerable disagreement in the literature as to just what armament *Komintern* had and when, where as a training ship it seems to have had a very unorthodox secondary weapons fit that included – during the 1930s – not only the relatively standard for the period 76.2mm (30.5 cal) Lender and 45mm (46 cal) 21-K anti-aircraft guns, but also aged 75mm (50 cal) Canet and 47mm (43.5 cal) Hotchkiss mounts from the pre-Soviet

The Bogatir'-class cruiser *Pamiat' Merkuriia* in Tsarist service. It would later become the *Komintern* in Soviet service. (Alamy)

period. These contrasted with more modern but unsuccessful Soviet 37mm Obr 1930 anti-aircraft mounts, possibly installed in the early 1930s, and 76.2mm (55 cal) 34-K mounts, reported to have been installed in place of Lender mounts at the very end of its career.

Pamiat' Merkuriia saw active combat service in the Black Sea during World War I with the Tsarist fleet before seeing similarly active service again in the Black Sea as *Komintern* with Soviet forces during the early stages of the Great Patriotic War. Against Turkish forces in the Black Sea during World War I, *Pamiat' Merkuriia* (often operating with its sister *Kagul*) was able to participate in the sort of cruiser operations for which the type was widely intended at the turn of the century, both operating with the fleet and more independently. Active operations continued after the February 1917 Revolution had brought the Provisional Government into nominal power in Russia, with its final operation before the Bolshevik Revolution in October taking place in August 1917 when it participated in an attack on the Turkish port of Ordu.

From September 1917, *Pamiat' Merkuriia* was based out of Odessa. Many of its crew were apparently Ukrainian, some with leanings towards the Central Ukrainian Rada in Kyiv – a fledgling Ukrainian government. Indeed, after the Bolshevik seizure of power in Petrograd, the cruiser raised the Ukrainian flag. It was subsequently embroiled in the struggle between Bolshevik forces and those loyal to the Ukrainian Rada, where ultimately at least part of its crew loyal to the Bolsheviks ended up raising the red flag of the Revolution and evacuated themselves and other Red supporters from Odessa to Sevastopol' with the ship in early 1918. Once in Sevastopol', it was declared to be a second-line vessel and put into storage – the state it was in when the port was subsequently occupied by German forces. *Pamiat' Merkuriia* was then used by German troops as a floating barracks. German forces were replaced by the British and French at the end of 1918, the British leaving Sevastopol' in late April 1919 – leaving behind *Pamiat' Merkuriia* but wrecking much of its machinery before they left. At this time, *Pamiat' Merkuriia* was therefore of little value to White forces that would take over control of Sevastopol'. By the time the Whites finally evacuated the region in late 1920, the cruiser was in a sorry state, having lost most of its armament (only the 152mm guns in its two turrets remaining) as well as the ability to move anywhere under its own steam.

Despite its dilapidated condition, *Pamiat' Merkuriia* would subsequently be restored by the Soviets, housing the headquarters for Soviet forces of the Black Sea and Sea of Azov in the late summer of 1921. Its machinery was repaired with help from some of its sister ships and other vessels – *Bogatir'* among them – and the main armament replaced with 130mm (55 cal) guns. By 1923, it was ready for working up with Soviet naval forces as *Komintern* – its new name from 1 May 1923 – before formally entering Soviet service later that year.

In November 1925, *Komintern* would play a starring role in Sergei Eisenstein's movie *Battleship Potemkin* – with many on-ship scenes in the film being shot on *Komintern* – and in late 1928 it conducted an overseas visit to Istanbul on the fifth anniversary of the ascendancy of the 'national-liberation' movement in Turkey.

Overhauled in 1930–31, it served for most of the 1930s as a training vessel, although in June 1941 during repairs it was re-equipped as a minelayer that entered service with the Black Sea Fleet on the second day of the Great Patriotic War, 23 June 1941.

Komintern at war, 1941–42

At the beginning of the Great Patriotic War, *Komintern* served in its new role as a minelayer – at the end of June 1941 alone laying more than 600 mines over a five-day period near Sevastopol'. During July, *Komintern* was based out of Odessa – laying more mines but also starting to engage in other types of work such as covering the retreat of the Soviet Danube Flotilla to Odessa. Indeed, by August, minelaying was already in *Komintern*'s past as it joined the

One of the distinguishing features of the Bogatir'-class cruisers was the distinctive cutaway of the deck at the bow – making identification of *Komintern* in this picture straightforward. Here, it is being led out of Odessa by a Novik-class destroyer in September 1941. (Getty)

many other Soviet warships involved in bringing in and evacuating men and materiel from Odessa and the Crimea. For example, on 16 and 17 September, *Komintern* was part of the escort for the transports *Dnepr* and *Abkhaziia* conveying men and materiel from Novorossiisk to Yalta in the Crimea. By 7 October, it was assisting in the evacuation of the besieged port of Odessa, carrying 1,455 personnel and 250 tonnes of supplies. After a brief period under repair at Poti, it was again ferrying supplies into Sevastopol' on 7 November and two days later would evacuate 500 civilians, 160 wounded and approximately 300 tonnes of naval ordnance to Poti. Such activities continued through to the following spring, when from 20 January to 11 March 1942 alone, *Komintern* would make four visits to Sevastopol' and deliver 1,926 troops, 649 tonnes of supplies, 18 vehicles and other equipment to the besieged city.

A dummy version of a Soviet KB moored contact mine. Both Tsarist Russia and the Soviet Union invested heavily in mine warfare, with cruisers being equipped to act as fast minelayers. The KB was a type of mine laid by both *Komintern* and *Marti* early in the Great Patriotic War. This example is in the Museum of the Northern Fleet in Murmansk, Russia. (AC)

Most Soviet vessels of the period of the Great Patriotic War – including eventually *Marti* and cruisers in this book – were provided with the ubiquitous 12.7mm DShK machine gun on a mount like this example in the Central Museum of the Armed Forces in Moscow. (AC)

Although *Komintern* was clearly carrying out a useful transport role, it was, by virtue of its age and limited wider value, relatively expendable. This is perhaps highlighted by a written order from the head of the Soviet Navy given on 9 September 1941, in which he suggested that the defences of Sevastopol' might be augmented using the guns from *Komintern* and a number of other vessels. *Komintern* would, however, end up keeping its armament into 1942.

By the spring of 1942, conditions for Soviet naval operations in the Black Sea – and even for bases well to the east – were increasingly dangerous in the face of German airpower. In late April, *Komintern* was damaged in a German bombing raid on Novorossiisk, then on 2 July it suffered 69 casualties after a direct hit. Evacuation to Poti did not mean the ship was safe – on 16 July, it again suffered a direct hit with an aerial bomb that failed to explode, but which nonetheless holed the ship. This particular air attack was significant enough to warrant a directive from the head of the Soviet Navy on the need for the dispersal of ships in port and to keep them at sea if possible.

In the face of the threat from German airpower and mounting damage – and the absence of suitable repair facilities – the decision was quickly taken by the command of the Black Sea Fleet to send *Komintern* further east to Tuapse with 500 troops on board – limited to a speed that did not exceed 8 knots – where, the same day as it arrived, it was stripped of seven 130mm, three 76.2mm, three 45mm and two 25mm guns, along with five 12.7mm machine guns. One hundred and eighty-four of *Komintern*'s crew would accompany these weapons and a rangefinder, subsequently being used to form six batteries covering the approaches to Tuapse. On 10 October 1942 – with all of its precious armament removed – *Komintern* was led by tug out of the harbour at Poti and sunk in shallow water as a breakwater at the mouth of the Khobi River. As such, *Komintern*'s remains would still be visible decades after being scuttled.

Cruisers of the Svetlana class

By the mid-1920s, the Soviet Navy had kept only two of the many completed cruisers it had inherited from its Tsarist predecessor – *Aurora* and *Komintern*. The Soviet Union had also, however, retained the hulls of all eight vessels of the incomplete Tsarist Svetlana class, ultimately completing two of them – *Profintern* and *Chervona Ukraina* – to specifications close to those originally intended, the former later renamed *Krasnii Krim*. These two vessels were joined by a third cruiser constructed on one of the Svetlana-class hulls – *Krasnii Kavkaz* – that was completed with more significant variance from the original plans than its two sister ships.

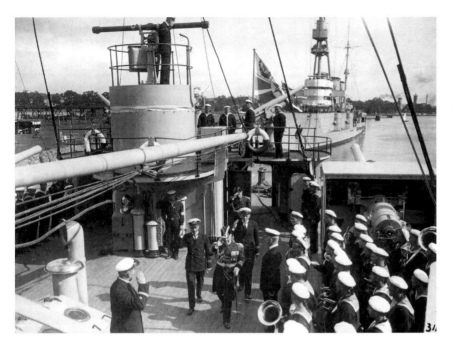

The newly constructed *Profintern* appears here behind the *Aurora* as the latter is being shown off to German guests at Swinemünde in Germany in August 1929. (Scherl/Süddeutsche Zeitung Photo/TopFoto)

All three vessels that would enter service with the Soviet Navy were laid down shortly before the outbreak of World War I – *Chervona Ukraina* (formerly *Admiral Nakhimov*) and *Krasnii Kavkaz* (formerly *Admiral Lazarev*) on 19 October 1913, and *Profintern* (formerly *Svetlana*) shortly afterwards on 24 November, the latter at Revel, the former two at Nikolaev on the Black Sea. This class of cruiser was to be constructed solely in Russian yards.

Svetlana was launched on 28 November 1915 at Revel, and was moved in incomplete state to Petrograd in late 1917 in the face of the danger of Revel falling to German forces. *Admiral Nakhimov* and *Admiral Lazarev* were launched on 24 October 1915 and 8 June 1916 respectively. With all three vessels incomplete when the Tsarist regime fell, the new Provisional Government called a halt to work on all of the vessels in April 1917. Soon the Provisional Government also fell, but it would not be until the end of the Civil War that the Bolsheviks would be in any position to do anything meaningful with the hulls. In the case of the two vessels being constructed on the Black Sea that would ultimately be completed by the Bolsheviks, the Bolsheviks were not actually in possession of the hulls for much of the Civil War period. In 1919, for example, *Admiral Nakhimov* – which would become *Chervona Ukraina* in Soviet service – was under the control of a short-lived Ukrainian government that renamed it *Get'man Bogdan Khmel'nits'kii*.

After the end of the Civil War, *Svetlana* kept its initial name, even after the Bolshevik government had in principle decided to complete it (and *Admiral Nakhimov*) during the period from late 1921 through to the summer of 1922 – only being renamed *Profintern* on 5 February 1925. By this point, work had finally started in earnest on completing the ship after it was moved to the Baltic Factory in what was now Leningrad in late 1924. Of the two Black Sea hulls, *Admiral Nakhimov* became *Chervona Ukraina* on 7 December 1922 before work to complete it nominally started the following spring.

Chervona Ukraina is photographed here at some point before the mid-1930s. Note the funnel bands on its two rear funnels as well as the prominent and somewhat outdated casemates for the secondary armament. (NH, 89391)

Krasnii Kavkaz was, as noted above, finished to a different specification to its sisters, work to complete it starting later – it would not be renamed (from *Admiral Lazarev*) until 14 December 1926, where back in the summer of 1922, when further decisions about the fate of the class were being taken, its completion had been put on hold pending suitable financial circumstances. Interestingly, the hulls of two other potential members of the class – *Admiral Greig* and *Admiral Spiridov* – were completed as tankers, with the remainder being scrapped.

After protracted periods to complete the vessels – nominally nearly seven years in the case of *Profintern* – the three light cruisers were completed as follows in Table 7. Note the slightly greater size of the Black Sea vessels.

Table 7: Soviet cruisers as completed using hulls of Svetlana-class vessels launched prior to 1917					
			Profintern	Chervona Ukraina	Krasnii Kavkaz
Entered service			1 July 1928	21 March 1927	25 January 1932
Displacement full load (tonnes)		normal load (tonnes)	6,887	7,600	7,600
			8,170	9,030	
Dimensions		Maximum length (m)	158.4	166.86	169.5
		Maximum width (m)	15.35	15.7	15.71
Draught (normal load) (m)			5.65	5.58	6.6
Speed (maximum) (kts)			29	29.8	29.5
Range (economical speed) (miles)			3,350	1,227	1,490
Armament*		Main	15x130mm (55 cal) (6 in casemates)	15x130mm (55 cal) (6 in casemates)	4x180mm (60 cal) MK-1-180
		Secondary	9x75mm (50 cal) Canet/Meller 4x7.62mm Maxim	8x75mm (50 cal) Canet/Meller	4x102mm (45 cal) B-2 4x12.7mm DK-32
		Torpedoes	2x450mm (below waterline) (3 x triple 450mm Obr 1913 intended)	2x450mm (below waterline) (3 x triple 450mm Obr 1913 intended)	4 x triple 450mm Obr 1913
Armoured protection	Belt (maximum)/deck (maximum)/bridge (maximum)/guns (maximum)		75/20/125/25mm	75/25/125/25mm	75/20/125/38mm
Crew			630	630	c 600

*All vessels were able to carry and lay up to 100 mines throughout their service careers

The principle modifications made to all three vessels of this class prior to and during World War II concerned their anti-aircraft armaments. All naval powers became aware as the conflict progressed that surface ships were extremely vulnerable to attack from the air, and the Soviet Navy was no exception. The anti-aircraft armaments of these vessels were first augmented with the 45mm 21-K semi-automatic gun before the subsequent addition of 37mm automatic 70-K weapons.

By 1944 (or in the case of *Chervona Ukraina* 1941), the displacements of all of the Svetlana-class cruisers had increased – largely due to additional anti-aircraft armament – with this and age contributing to lower maximum speeds and ranges than when they first entered service, as noted in Table 8.

Table 8: Wartime specifications for cruisers of the Svetlana class

	Krasnii Krim (formerly *Profintern*) (1944)	*Chervona Ukraina* (1941)	*Krasnii Kavkaz* (1944)
Displacement (normal load) (tonnes)	7,190	8,400 (full)	c 8,000
Draught (normal load) (m)	5.77	6.2 (full)	5.96
Speed (maximum) (kts)	22	27.5	29
Range (economical speed) (miles)	1,230	2,700	1,490
Crew	852	830	878
Augmented wartime AA armament	3 x twin 100mm (47 cal) 'Minizin' 4x45mm (46 cal) 21-K 10x37mm (67.5 cal) 70-K 4x12.7mm DShK 2 x quad 12.7mm Vickers HMG	3 x twin 100mm (47 cal) 'Minizin' 6x45mm (46 cal) 21-K up to 7x12.7mm DShK	6 x twin 100mm (47 cal) 'Minizin' 2x76mm (55 cal) 34-K 4x45mm (46 cal) 21-K 10x37mm (67.5 cal) 70-K 6x12.7mm DShK 2 x quad 12.7mm Vickers HMG
Wartime torpedo armament	2 x triple 533mm 39-iu	4 x triple 450mm Obr 1913	4 x triple 450mm Obr 1913

Chervona Ukraina, *Krasnii Krim* and *Krasnii Kavkaz* at war, 1941–45

The three vessels of the former Tsarist Svetlana class had active wartime careers, with *Chervona Ukraina* having the unfortunate distinction of being the only Soviet cruiser lost outright to enemy action during the war.

At the beginning of the Great Patriotic War of the Soviet Union on 22 June 1941, all three of these cruisers were part of the Soviet Black Sea Fleet's 'Cruiser Brigade' (with the Type 26 and 26-bis cruisers, *Voroshilov* and *Molotov*, in a separate 'Light Forces Detachment'). The 'Cruiser Brigade'

An early shot of the front section of *Krasnii Kavkaz* taken in 1933, not long after its completion. Particularly prominent are the four single 102mm 45-calibre B-2 guns for secondary armament – another dimension, in addition to the four 180mm 60-calibre guns that were its main armament, in which it was unique amongst Soviet cruisers. (NH, 86807)

On this rear section of *Krasnii Kavkaz*, in a photograph taken at the same time as the previous image in 1933, note the prominent red star on one of its main turrets. Such embellishments were very typical of the early 1930s during a period in which revolutionary symbolism accompanied rapid social and economic change. (NH, 86808)

would play a significant role in the defence of the port of Odessa in the face of advancing Rumanian forces during the summer of 1941, with *Krasnii Krim* being the first of the cruisers of the force to bring reinforcements to the beleaguered city from its home base at Sevastopol' on 21 August 1941. Together with the destroyers *Dzerzhinskii* and *Frunze* (see NVG 256), it brought in 1,300 reinforcements for Odessa. While at Odessa, *Krasnii Krim* was attacked by enemy aircraft – the first combat for this class of vessel. On its return to Sevastopol', it was engaged in the shore bombardment of Rumanian forces outside Odessa, reaching Sevastopol' on 24 August.

As the Axis assault on Odessa continued, the Soviet cruisers would play an important role in providing artillery support to the defenders. At the end of August, it was the turn of *Chervona Ukraina* to do so, initially along with the destroyer leader *Tashkent* and destroyers *Frunze* and *Smishlenii*. The importance of this fire-support role is highlighted by the fact that by 31 August, a small armada of Soviet warships was providing fire support for Soviet forces on the eastern flank of the attack on Odessa, including not only *Chervona Ukraina*, but also *Komintern*, four destroyers (*Dzerzhinskii*, *Nezamozhnik*, *Frunze* and *Shaumian*) and two gunboats (*Krasnaia Armeniia* and *Krasnaia Gruziia*). In early September, it was *Krasnii Kavkaz*'s turn to provide fire support off Odessa, by which time all three of the Svetlana-class vessels had taken their turn.

During this first period of the war, these cruisers were used in increasingly bold ways as the Soviets made effective use of their naval superiority to exploit their seaward flank in the Black Sea (even if that superiority could not change the course of events on land). On 22 September, a sizeable Soviet naval force, including both *Krasnii Kavkaz* and *Krasnii Krim*, supported

D

CHERVONA UKRAINA AND *KRASNII KRIM* (SVETLANA CLASS)

The first cruisers to be completed under Soviet power were the Svetlana-class vessels *Chervona Ukraina* and *Profintern* (later renamed *Krasnii Krim*). Both cruisers had been launched under the Tsarist regime, and were completed by the Soviet Union in the late 1920s in forms close to those originally intended. *Chervona Ukraina* is shown here as completed in 1927 with a main armament of 15 130mm (55 cal) guns and secondary armament of only eight 75mm (50 cal) dual-purpose guns and two machine guns. Its sister ship, *Krasnii Krim*, is shown in its late 1943 form with significantly augmented anti-aircraft armament compared to the paltry armament these vessels started with when completed. Here, *Krasnii Krim* has, in addition to three twin 100mm (47 cal) 'Minizin' mounts and four 45mm (46 cal) 21-K semi-automatics, a powerful ten-gun complement of 37mm (67.5 cal) automatics, two quad 12.7mm Vickers mounts and four single 12.7mm DShK heavy machine guns. Note also *Krasnii Krim*'s torpedo armament.

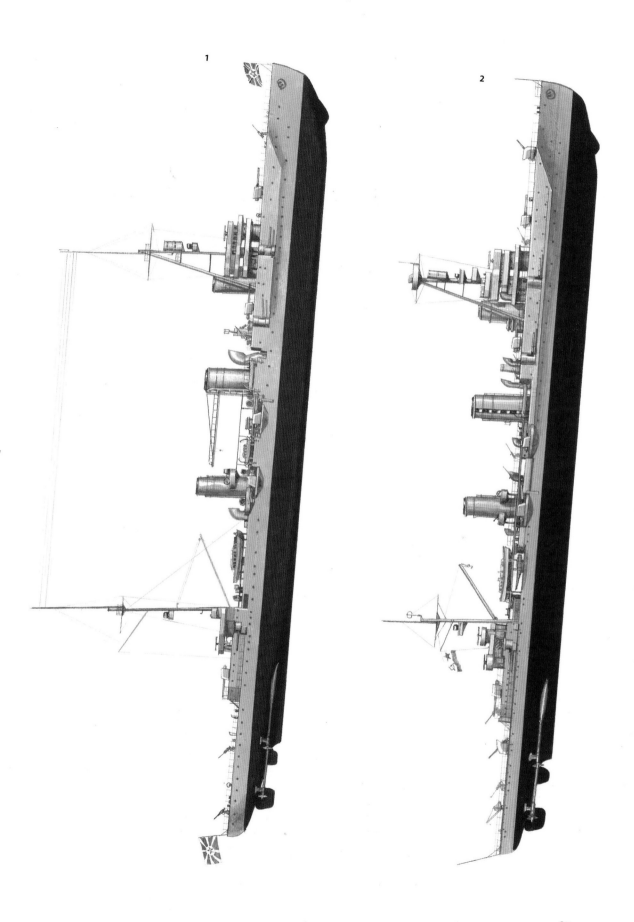

1

2

Another shot of *Krasnii Kavkaz* taken somewhat later, during the second half of the 1930s, in which once again the vessel has red stars added to its paintwork for some sort of festivities, this time to funnels. Note that in this picture, it now has twin 100mm guns aft of the bridge structure, losing the B-2 guns further aft. (NH, 71486)

a Soviet naval landing on the eastern flank of the Axis attack on Odessa. When the situation at Odessa became unsustainable by mid-October, the cruisers would on 16 October play their part in evacuating some of the defenders of the city (1,164 in the case of *Chervona Ukraina* and 1,127 for *Krasnii Kavkaz*).

After taking Odessa, Axis forces would soon move on by October 1941 to threaten Sevastopol'. In the context of that threat, the decision was taken to move those Soviet warships deemed most valuable further east to the Caucasus, leaving *Krasnii Krim* and *Chervona Ukraina* in Sevastopol' along with a number of destroyers. Hence, on 1 November 1941, the battleship *Parizhkaia kommuna*, cruisers *Molotov*, *Voroshilov* and *Krasnii Kavkaz*, the destroyer leader *Tashkent* and other vessels left Sevastopol'. *Krasnii Kavkaz* no doubt left not because of its value, but because of limitations in the use of its main armament noted below. Leaving the two other light cruisers at Sevastopol' undoubtedly facilitated its defence, their guns providing meaningful fire support in mid-November as Axis forces sought to storm the city – *Chervona Ukraina* firing around 700 rounds of 130mm ammunition on 11 November alone. The following day, however, *Chervona Ukraina* would fire its last salvoes, a near miss by a 250kg bomb from an attacking Heinkel 111 causing a fire and significant damage. Although that fire was extinguished, German aviation continued to attack the cruiser, Heinkel 111s followed by Ju 87 Stukas and then more Heinkels – by which time only one twin 100mm, two 45mm and two AA machine guns remained in operation to defend the ship. Further air attacks and near misses caused additional damage to the vessel, which had already taken on significant water, and by the small hours of 13 November the removal of *Chervona Ukraina*'s armament in the face of the prospect of its loss was well advanced. With its list increasing rapidly – from 6.5 per

In this photograph, then Vice-Admiral Filipp Oktiabr'skii, commanding the Soviet Black Sea Fleet, reviews the crew of the cruiser *Krasnii Kavkaz* in July 1940. (NH, 71485)

cent at midnight to 9 per cent at 0200hrs and 11 per cent at 0300hrs on 13 November – its fate was clear, and at 0330hrs, with a list of 25 per cent, the decision was taken to abandon ship. It wasn't long before the vessel had keeled over onto its left side in shallow water. It would not be raised until 1947, and it was subsequently scrapped.

Because the Soviets' superiority in naval power in the region was such a significant asset, *Chervona Ukraina*'s loss did not stop the intensive exploitation of Soviet naval forces in the Black Sea – it being particularly valuable where the fate of Sevastopol' was in

Troops board the *Krasnii Kavkaz* for one of the many runs of the cruisers of the class into besieged ports during the first year of the Great Patriotic War. Note the DShK heavy machine gun at the top of the picture. (MacLaren/Sovfoto)

the balance. For example, in the face of a second attempt to seize Sevastopol' by Axis forces in December on the 20th of that month, the 79th Naval Rifle Brigade was dispatched to the city by sea to bolster its defences, using the cruisers *Krasnii Kavkaz* and *Krasnii Krim*, along with the destroyer *Bodrii* and destroyer leader *Tashkent*.

Krasnii Kavkaz and *Krasnii Krim* would subsequently play an important role in the Soviet Kerch'-Feodosiia landings at the end of December 1941. These landings on the eastern part of the Crimean peninsula were intended to relieve the siege of Sevastopol' and liberate the Crimea. Although the Soviet force concerned would ultimately be destroyed in May 1942, the naval landings at the port of Feodosiia in which the two light cruisers were involved went successfully and highlighted the potential that Soviet command of the sea provided. On 28 December 1941, *Krasnii Kavkaz* embarked 1,586 troops, six 76mm guns, two mortars and 15 light vehicles for the landings, with *Krasnii Krim* adding approximately 2,000 troops, two mortars, 53 tonnes of munitions and 18 tonnes of foodstuffs. Just how much was being carried by the two vessels for the landings is highlighted by the fact that *Krasnii Kavkaz*'s draught was temporarily 6.4m at the bow and 6.55m at the stern, with the corresponding figures for *Krasnii Krim* being 6.41m and 6.31m. Both cruisers were hit numerous times during the daring landings at the port and provided valuable fire support – *Krasnii Kavkaz* fired up to 13 180mm, 429 100mm and 472 45mm rounds during only a few hours, with *Krasnii Krim* adding 318 130mm and 472 45mm rounds.

This wartime picture shows one of the quad Vickers heavy machine guns that were added to both *Krasnii Kavkaz* and *Krasnii Krim* in 1941–42 as part of augmentation of their AA armament. (MacLaren/Sovfoto)

During further runs to the Crimea, both in support of the landings and the defence and evacuation of Sevastopol' during 1942, *Krasnii Krim* avoided significant damage. After participating in the evacuation of Novorossiisk later that summer and further operations along the coastline of the Caucasus into 1943, its wartime activities were wound down, and in March 1945 it became a training vessel. The intensity with which it had been used during the war is perhaps best highlighted by the fact that in that time it expended 3,156 rounds of ammunition from its main armament.

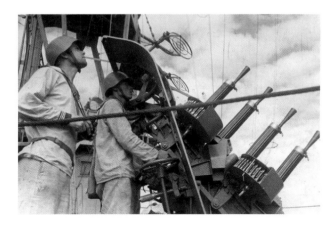

Crew members of *Krasnii Kavkaz* pose before one of its twin 100mm 'Minizin' mounts in April 1942. While the naval personnel obscure some of the mount, it is important not to forget that the cruisers covered in this book were crewed by hundreds of such sailors. (MacLaren/Sovfoto)

Krasnii Kavkaz was not quite as fortunate as *Krasnii Krim*. In early January 1942 – having transported the 224th Independent Anti-Aircraft Divizion to Feodosiia – it was attacked by Axis aircraft and as a result of five near misses took on 1,000 tonnes of water and had to be towed to Tuapse. Repairs took until late summer, but did mean the ship's AA armament was augmented, so by 1944 it had ten 37mm 70-K automatics (losing two quad M-4s that were replaced with 2x4 12.7mm Vickers mounts), also receiving an additional two 100mm 'Minizin' mounts from *Chervona Ukraina*. The remainder of *Krasnii Kavkaz*'s wartime career was similar to that of *Krasnii Krim*, emerging in May 1945 from a period of repair that had begun in September 1944. Problems with *Krasnii Kavkaz*'s MK-1-180 turrets with B-1-K guns meant that it had not made much use of its main armament during the war, the life of each barrel being exceedingly short and replacements not being forthcoming. As a result, it only fired 458 rounds from its main armament during the whole war.

Both *Krasnii Krim* and *Krasnii Kavkaz* received the 'Guards' designation during the war in recognition of their service.

Marti (formerly *Shtandart*)

Included in this book by virtue of its tonnage, armament, active service, novelty and indeed by the fact that it was laid down as a cruiser of sorts, is the Soviet minelayer *Marti*, formerly Tsar Nicholas II's royal yacht *Shtandart*.

Shtandart was laid down in Copenhagen prior to October 1893 as a vessel for the Russian *dobrovol'nii flot* – a state-controlled maritime transport organisation – with the potential to serve as an auxiliary (or *vspomogatel'nii*) cruiser should that be required. The ship was nominally laid down a second time on 1 October 1893 after Nicholas II had decided that the vessel would become the future royal yacht *Shtandart*. It was subsequently launched on 26 February 1895 and entered service as the royal yacht the following year. Its statistics as constructed are provided in Table 9.

KRASNII KAVKAZ (SVETLANA CLASS) DURING THE SUMMER OF 1942

All three of the Soviet cruisers completed from Tsarist Svetlana-class hulls saw active service in support of besieged Soviet ports on the Black Sea, including the atypical variant, *Krasnii Kavkaz*. This vessel had the misfortune of being provided with four 180mm (60 cal) MK-1-180 mounts for its main armament – the short barrel lives of which and lack of replacements meant that it made relatively little use of the main armament during the war. *Krasnii Kavkaz* is shown here sometime in mid-1942, loading with troops and equipment. Repairs during the winter of 1941–42 and additions into 1942 saw its anti-aircraft armament substantially augmented. As shown here, it not only has two additional twin 100mm (47 cal) 'Minizin' mounts taken from *Chervona Ukraina* to give it a total of six, but now has two single 76mm (55 cal) 34-K mounts added at the stern. The ship has also received ten 37mm (67.5 cal) 70-K automatic mounts to go with six semi-automatic (46 cal) 45-K mounts and a pair of quad Vickers HMG mounts. Loading using one of its aircraft cranes is a 76.2mm Obr. 1939 divisional artillery piece (USV).

This shot of *Krasnii Krim* in mid-1943 is taken from the stern looking forward to a twin 100mm 'Minizin' mount below a single 130mm mount. (NH, 86795)

Table 9: Specifications for the royal yacht *Shtandart* – the future minelayer *Marti* – as completed

Displacement	Normal (tonnes)	5,400
	Full (tonnes)	6,189
Dimensions	Maximum length (m)	128
	Maximum width (m)	15.4
Draught (m)		(bow) 5.8, (stern) 6.6
Speed	(maximum) (kts)	22
Armament	(Saluting guns)	8x47mm (43.5 cal) Hotchkiss
Armoured protection	None	
Crew		355

After having been used by the Tsar prior to World War I, *Shtandart* was used as a transport ship during 1915 and 1916, running between Kronstadt and Helsingfors. At the time of the February Revolution in 1917, it was in port at Petrograd. In mid-July 1917 – now officially the 'former' royal yacht – it departed for Helsingfors. *Shtandart* would subsequently return to Russian waters (and Kronstadt) after the Brest-Litovsk peace treaty with Germany of 3 March 1918 forced Russian vessels from ports in Finland and Estonia. By this point, *Shtandart* had been – at least unofficially – renamed *18 March* at the request of its crew, the date being that for the first day of the existence of the Paris Commune in 1871.

Having considered using *Shtandart* as a base ship for submarines or a transport for motor torpedo boats, for many years the vessel languished in unmodified form in reserve before the decision was finally taken to convert it into a minelayer – a conversion for which it was well suited. On 31 October 1931, the Soviet Navy finalized plans for its conversion, which was due to be completed by the summer of 1933. The conversion turned out to be more complicated to implement than anticipated, and plans were revised in September 1933 after it was supposed to already have been converted.

Krasnii Krim taken somewhere around 1943, and showing a triple torpedo tube mount aft of two of its 130mm gun mounts. (NH, 86798)

The conversion was finally completed – and the vessel entered service with the Baltic Fleet as *Marti* – on 25 December 1936. It was initially armed with four 130mm (55 cal) Obukhov mounts for its main gun armament, along with seven 76mm (30.5 cal) Lender AA guns, three 45mm (46 cal) semi-automatic 21-K mounts and four 7.62mm machine guns. It also initially had the capacity to carry and lay up to 523 mines (Obr 1912).

Marti at war, 1939–45

During the Soviet-Finnish War of late 1939 and early 1940, *Marti* was involved in its first combat mission laying mines off Finland. After the Baltic Republics were incorporated into the Soviet Union in 1940, *Marti* would be based out of Liepāja and Tallinn. It was from there during the first days of the Great Patriotic War that it would lay mines in the Gulf of Finland.

Krasnii Krim looking aft and showing all armament. Particularly clear in this photograph are some of the vessel's boats. (NH, 86800)

The Russian royal yacht *Shtandart* shown here prior to World War I. Its conversion into the Soviet minelayer *Marti* would dramatically transform the ship's appearance. (NH, 101022)

During the night of 23/24 June 1941, *Marti* and fellow minelayer *Ural* – protected by the destroyer leaders *Leningrad* and *Minsk* and destroyers *Iakov Sverdlov*, *Artem*, *Karl Marx* and *Volodarskii*, along with aircraft of the Baltic Fleet – would lay the first of many mines to protect Soviet waters and bases. By early August, as German forces threatened Tallinn, *Marti* was ordered to move to Kronstadt.

Most of the vessels that had joined *Marti* in the minelaying sortie of 23/24 June mentioned above had by early September been sunk, and *Marti* itself would suffer a number of near misses by German bombs in late September 1941, although it was able to lay more mines before the end of the month. *Marti* would subsequently participate in the evacuation of Soviet forces from Khanko in late October, *en route* to which the ship struck a mine and suffered significant damage. Despite this damage, *Marti* was still able to participate in the evacuation, successfully transporting 2,029 personnel, 60 'weapons pieces' and munitions of the 343rd Artillery Regiment and 270th Rifle Regiment from Khanko.

During the winter of 1941–42, *Marti* was, like many vessels of the Baltic Fleet, stuck in Leningrad (quite literally, given the ice), moored and camouflaged but still subject to enemy air attack. It nonetheless survived the ordeal and was awarded, on 3 April 1942, the title of 'Guards' – the crew receiving the appropriate flag on 5 September 1942. During 1943, *Marti* was involved in a short mission to suppress a German artillery battery located in a park in German-occupied Pavlovsk, but otherwise saw little activity other than training and continued to be under repair. It would ultimately be expended as a target before scrapping. *Marti*'s statistics for 1943 are provided in Table 10.

THE MINELAYER *MARTI*, FORMERLY THE ROYAL YACHT *SHTANDART*

The cruiser-sized minelayer *Marti* saw intensive service in the Baltic during the early part of the Great Patriotic War. Based on the hull of the former imperial yacht *Shtandart*, the *Marti* underwent a fairly dramatic conversion into a minelayer during the mid-1930s. It appears here as it looked early in the Great Patriotic War. The vessel retains its initial main armament of four 130mm (55 cal) Obukhov mounts and three 45mm (46 cal) semi-automatic 21-K mounts for AA defence, but has lost its World War I-vintage 76mm (30.5 cal) Lender anti-aircraft guns with which it was initially armed, which have been replaced with seven of the far more effective single 76mm (55 cal) 34-K mounts. At this point of the war, its machine-gun armament still consisted of 7.62mm Maxims rather than the 12.7mm DShKs added later.

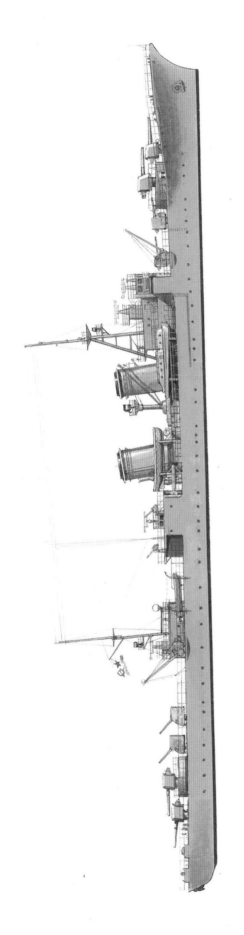

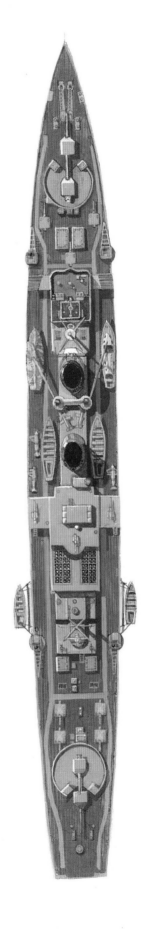

Table 10: The minelayer *Marti*'s specifications in 1943

Displacement	Normal (tonnes)	5,980
	Full (tonnes)	6,189
Dimensions	Maximum length (m)	122.3
	Maximum width (m)	15.39
Draught (m)		6.97
Speed	(maximum) (kts)	18
	While laying mines (maximum) (kts)	18
Range	At 14 knots (miles)	990
	At 12 knots (miles)	2,260
Armament	Main	4x130mm (55 cal)
	Secondary	7x76mm 34-K (55 cal), 3x45mm 21-K (46 cal), 2x12.7mm DShK HMG, 1x12.7mm Vickers HMG
	Mines	Up to 416 (depending on type)
Armoured protection	bridge (maximum)/gun shields (maximum)	12mm/70mm
Crew		578

CRUISERS LAID DOWN AND COMPLETED 1917–45

Cruisers of the Kirov class (Project 26 and Project 26-bis)

Having completed three cruisers of the Svetlana class that were inherited in incomplete states from the Tsarist regime, by the mid-1930s Soviet industry was in a far better position to design and build its own cruisers than it had been less than a decade before. By this time, Soviet industry was under increasing pressure to do so as Soviet leader Stalin sought to build up an 'ocean-going' fleet fitting for a growing power like the Soviet Union. If other powers were building cruisers, then the Soviet Union needed them too. During the 2nd Five-Year Plan for Soviet industry of the early–mid-1930s, the Soviet Union was at one point supposed to build a staggering eight new cruisers – a task well beyond Soviet capabilities but typical of the hyperbole of the state's plans during that time.

As with the destroyer leader *Tashkent* (see NVG 256, pp.42–43), the Soviet Union sought foreign assistance in the construction of its new cruisers. At this time, the Soviet Union still lagged behind foreign competitors in terms of higher technologies – and it had never built a warship of anything like such size from scratch. Although plans to acquire a completed first cruiser from Italy did not come to fruition, the power plant for the lead cruiser of a new type – the Type 26 or Kirov class – was purchased there. Italian influence over the Soviet design is apparent when the lines of the Kirov class are compared to Italian light cruisers of the 1930s such as *Raimondo Montecuccoli*. Italian input did not prevent *Kirov*'s development from suffering many teething troubles that were shared by its sister *Voroshilov* – and to some extent ameliorated in the later derivative Project 26-bis vessels

The Italian light cruiser *Raimondo Montecuccoli*, commissioned in 1935, is shown here in 1938. When comparing it with photos of the Soviet Kirov class, the influence of Italian design on the Soviet vessels is very apparent. (State Library of Victoria)

Maksim Gor'kii, *Molotov* and *Kalinin*. One of the most noticeable of these is the fact that the Project 26 vessels were noticeably 'down in the bow'. The ironing-out of teething troubles was not helped by the fact that from the second half of 1936, the Great Purge was in progress and inadequacies in the cruiser construction programme inevitably attracted negative attention. Of the 'improved' Project 26-bis vessels, *Kaganovich* was also completed before the end of the war, raising the Soviet naval ensign on 23 February 1945 as part of the Pacific Fleet, but it and sister ship *Kalinin* would play no role in the war against Japan.

The vessels of the Project 26 and 26-bis were completed as in Table 11. Table 12 provides sample specifications for examples of the Project 26 and 26-bis vessels as completed.

The Project 26 cruiser *Kirov* shown at Kronstadt prior to the Great Patriotic War. (NH, 74285)

Table 11: Vessels of the Kirov class (Project 26 and 26-bis)

Vessel	Project	Laid Down	Launched	Entered service	Fleet
Kirov	26	11.10.1935	30.11.1936	26.09.1938	Baltic
Voroshilov	26	15.10.1935	26.07.1937	20.06.1940	Black Sea
Maksim Gor'kii	26-bis	20.12.1936	30.04.1938	12.11.1940	Baltic
Molotov	26-bis	14.01.1937	19.03.1939	14.06.1941	Black Sea
Kalinin	26-bis	12.06.1938	08.05.1942	31.12.1942 (nominally)	Pacific
Kaganovich	26-bis	26.08.1938	06.05.1944	30.12.1944 (nominally)	Pacific

Table 12: Specifications for examples of Kirov-class vessels (Project 26 and 26-bis) as completed

		Kirov (1938)	*Maksim Gor'kii* (1940)	*Kalinin* (1942)
Displacement (normal load) (tonnes)		8,540	8,882	9,105
Dimensions	Maximum length (m)	191.3	191.4	191.2
	Maximum width (m)	17.7	17.7	17.7
Draught (normal load) (m)		5.75	5.87	5.88
Speed (maximum) (kts)		36	36.1	36
Range (economical speed) (miles)		3,750	4,880	5,590
Armament	Main	3x3 180mm (57 cal) MK-3-180		
	Secondary	6x100mm (56 cal) B-34 6x45mm (46 cal) 21-K, 4x12.7mm DShK	6x100mm (56 cal) B-34 9x45mm (46 cal) 21-K 4x12.7mm DShK	8x85mm (52 cal) 90-K (after working up) 6x45mm (46 cal) 21-K 10x37mm (67.5 cal) 70-K 6x12.7mm DShK
	Torpedoes	2 x triple 533mm 39-iu		
Armoured protection	Belt (maximum)	50mm	70mm	70mm
	deck (maximum)	50mm	50mm	50mm
	bridge (maximum)	150mm	150mm	150mm
	turrets (maximum)	50mm	70mm	70mm
Crew		692	898	812

In the light of wartime experience, the anti-aircraft armaments of vessels of the two projects were significantly augmented, as is apparent in Table 13 that provides details for their armament, along with other related specifications late in the Great Patriotic War.

Table 13: Late-war specifications for selected Kirov-class (Project 26 and 26-bis) vessels

		Kirov (1944)	*Voroshilov* (1944)	*Maksim Gor'kii* (1944)	*Kalinin* (1945)
Displacement (normal load) (tonnes)		8,590	8,675	8,882	9,105
Speed (maximum) (kts)		35.94	34	36.1	32.5
Range (economical speed) (miles)		3,750	2,140	4,220	
Armament	**Main**	3x 3x180mm (57 cal) MK-3-180			
	Secondary	8x100mm (56 cal) B-34 10x37mm (67.5 cal) 70-K 4x12.7mm DShK 2x 4xVickers MG	6x100mm (56 cal) B-34 6x45mm (46 cal) 21-K 14x37mm (67.5 cal) 70-K 6x12.7mm DShK 2x 4xVickers MG	6x100mm (56 cal) B-34 Up to 15x37mm (67.5 cal) 70-K 6x12.7mm DShK 2x 4xVickers MG	8x85mm (52 cal) 90-K 19x37mm (67.5 cal) 70-K 6x12.7mm DShK
	Torpedoes	2x3 533mm 39-iu			
Crew		872	881	963	812

RADAR

When the Great Patriotic War started on 22 June 1941, the Project 26-bis cruiser *Molotov* was the only Soviet warship with any sort of radar – a Soviet *Redut* set. Prior to November 1941, *Molotov*'s radar was a – if not the – key element in Sevastopol's air defence system. By 1944, all other vessels of the class had received British (281, 282, 284, 285 and 291), US (SG) or Soviet sets, as in Table 14.

Table 14: Radar sets installed on Kirov-class vessels, 1944

Vessel	Search radar	Fire-control radar (main armament)	Fire-control radar (AA armament)
Kirov	291	284 and 2x285	2x282
Voroshilov	281	284 and 2x285	2x282
Maksim Gor'kii	291	284 and 2x285	2x282
Molotov	Redut-K	Mars-1	
Kalinin	281, SG	2x lupiter-1	2x282

Wartime service – Project 26 and 26-bis

The Project 26 and 26-bis vessels *Kirov*, *Molotov*, *Maksim Gor'kii* and *Voroshilov* all saw meaningful wartime service, with *Kirov* even seeing limited service during the Soviet-Finnish War of 1939–40 – firing 35 rounds from its 180mm guns at a Finnish island-based coastal battery on 1 December 1939. *Kirov* would go on to fire 235 rounds from its main armament in defence of the port of Tallinn in August 1941 before being evacuated to Kronstadt as part of the famous 'Tallinn passage' evacuation of Soviet naval forces at the end of that month. Although *Kirov* made it to Kronstadt – despite considerable danger from mines and air attack – many other Soviet vessels were lost, including the Type 7 destroyer *Skorii* and five Novik-class vessels (see NVG 256). From firstly Kronstadt and then Leningrad (where Soviet vessels were less exposed to German air

attack), *Kirov* was able to use its main armament against German forces advancing on the city despite taking damage from German bombs. In doing so it was joined by its Type 26-bis sister *Maksim Gor'kii*, which had the misfortune of losing its bow to a mine on only the second day of the war, but was able to get back to Tallinn and from there to Kronstadt, where the bow had been repaired by the beginning of August (and during which process its AA armament was augmented). *Maksim Gor'kii* too was subsequently transferred to Leningrad, where it and its sister would spend much of the war.

While Leningrad was safer for *Kirov* and *Maksim Gor'kii* than Kronstadt, the two vessels still constituted desirable targets for German aviation and long-range artillery – particularly as their firepower was a considerable

A wartime view of the main armament of a Kirov-class vessel looking aft. Note the paravanes on davits either side of the B mount used to provide a limited sweeping capability against mines. (NH, 100194)

The Project 26 cruiser *Voroshilov* shown in the Black Sea during the Great Patriotic War. (NH, 95504)

adjunct to the defences of the city. Heavy German air attacks in April 1942 would see *Kirov* take significant damage, leading to two months of repairs – during which it too would receive augmented AA defences. Having spent 1942 and 1943 as part of the defences of Leningrad, the two cruisers were in January 1944 assigned to provide fire support for Soviet offensive operations near Leningrad that would mean an end to the period of siege that the city had endured since September 1941. *Kirov* and *Maksim Gor'kii* would

A second and impressive wartime view of the Project 26 vessel *Voroshilov* in port in the relatively warm waters of the Black Sea. (MacLaren/Sovfoto)

The wartime augmentation of the AA armament on the Kirov class saw the addition of many 37mm 70-K automatic guns to vessels of the class, including this exposed gun on a B turret. (MacLaren/Sovfoto)

go on to provide fire support against Finnish forces during Soviet offensive operations in Karelia in June 1944.

For the remainder of the war, the two vessels would remain in Leningrad – Soviet naval commanders not wanting to jeopardize their careers losing a major surface vessel in the dangerous waters of the Baltic. Just how dangerous those waters were – even after the war – is highlighted by the fact that *Kirov* took considerable damage from an unswept mine not far from Kronstadt at around midnight on 16/17 October 1945.

The Project 26 and 26-bis vessels in the Black Sea saw more sustained active service than their counterparts in the Baltic. Prior to being heavily

damaged in an air attack on 2 November 1941 while at Novorossiisk, the *Voroshilov* had been active since the second day of the war when it was part of a force dispatched to shell Constanza. *Voroshilov* was based out of Sevastopol' until 25 September, after which it was moved to Novorossiisk for safety. *Voroshilov* – like other Soviet warships – was clearly still not safe in Novorossiisk, where it was hit by two aerial bombs during an air attack on 2 November 1941 that would force it to Poti for repairs. Back with the fleet by mid-March 1942, *Voroshilov*'s service history for the remainder of the year and into 1943 was one of active operations that included troop-carrying and fire support punctuated by brief periods of repair in June and early July 1942 and from December 1942 to January 1943. Despite emerging from repair in late January 1943, it would only carry out one more significant operation, at the very end of that month, which was to shell German positions near Novorossiisk. For the remainder of the war, it was based in Poti and Batumi.

G **KIROV AND MAKSIM GOR'KII (PROJECT 26 AND PROJECT 26-BIS)**
This illustration provides profiles of examples of both the Project 26 and Project 26-bis variants of what is widely known as the Kirov class. The lead Project 26 vessel, *Kirov*, is shown in its 1939 state shortly after completion, with the Project 26-bis vessel *Maksim Gor'kii* also shown not long after completion, in its case in 1941. Notable differences include both the bridge and main mast detail and secondary armament. *Maksim Gor'kii* is shown with nine 45mm (46 cal) 21-K semi-automatic anti-aircraft guns, compared to the *Kirov*'s six. Both otherwise have 6x100mm (56 cal) B-34 guns and four 12.7mm DShK heavy machine guns alongside their main armament consisting of three 180mm (57 cal) MK-3-180 mounts. As the war progressed, both vessels would see their AA armaments heavily augmented.

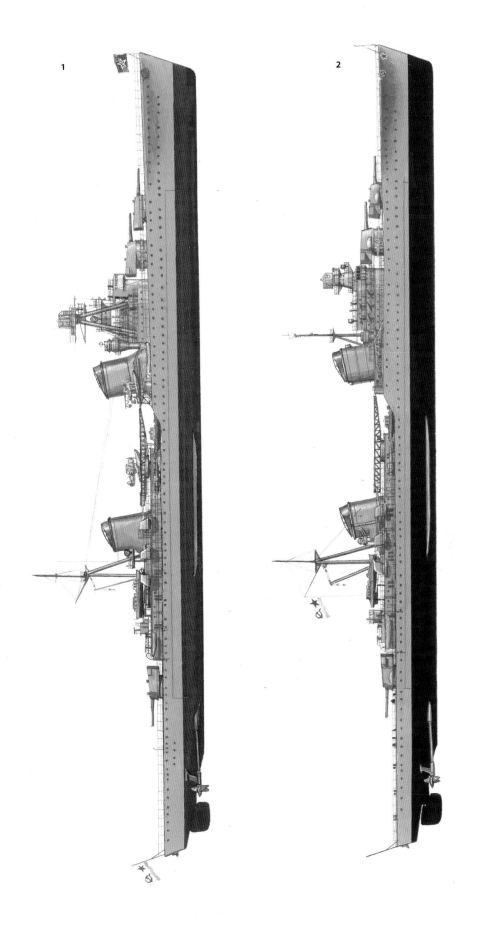

1

2

The Project 26-bis cruiser *Molotov* spent the first months of the war in port in Sevastopol', where its radar played a key part in the city's air defences, before being moved to Poti. From Poti it would make regular trips to the besieged city of Sevastopol'. Hit by what some sources claim was a German aerial torpedo during the night of 2/3 August 1942 – in Italian sources claimed to have been a torpedo from the MTB MAS 573 – the ship was able to get back to Poti, where it was under repair for nine months, a complex repair process involving fitting to it the stern section from the incomplete Project 68 (Chapaev-class) cruiser *Frunze*. This work was completed by April 1943, and *Molotov* rejoined the fleet at the end of July. As in the Baltic, there was little desire to risk the cruisers unnecessarily as the war progressed. This was particularly so after the loss of the destroyer leader *Khar'kov* and destroyers *Besposhchadnii* and *Sposobnii* to enemy air attack on their return to Tuapse after having shelled enemy positions at Feodosiia and Yalta in the Crimea on 6 October 1943 (see NVG 256, p.27).

Few in the crowd witnessing the launch of the German pocket battleship *Lützow* in 1939 could have imagined that it would soon serve as a floating battery in Soviet hands as *Petropavlovsk*, later being renamed *Tallinn*. (Getty)

Vessels of the Kirov class would continue to serve in the Soviet Navy into the 1970s before being finally disposed of.

Petropavlovsk (Lützow)

Under the auspices of the Nazi-Soviet Pact signed in August 1939, the Soviet Union sought to acquire German military technology. The most significant single acquisition for the Soviet Union was the German heavy cruiser *Lützow* – initially renamed *Petropavlovsk* in Soviet service. Laid down on 18 July 1936 in Bremen, Germany, it was launched on 1 July 1939 as *Lützow* (a name given after its sale to the Soviets to the light cruiser *Deutschland*). According to the subsequent agreement, the ship was to be delivered to the Soviet Union in partially completed state, with work then finished using German-supplied armament and equipment.

Whether the Soviet Union got value for money out of this deal is highly debatable. Although construction of *Petropavlovsk* in Leningrad initially went to plan, it was not long before the Germans were dragging their feet on the supply of the necessary armament and equipment to finish the project.

According to one Soviet officer who participated in its construction, by the spring of 1941 it was obvious that the German side was stalling, particularly where the delivery of armament was concerned.

Petropavlovsk at war, 1941–45

By the beginning of the Great Patriotic War, the cruiser was approximately 70 per cent complete, and even had most of its crew (all of the officers and senior ratings, and 60 per cent of the ratings). Germany had supplied ammunition for its main guns and anti-aircraft armament, but it was only fit to be prepared for service as a floating battery, not as a fully worked-up vessel. Table 15 provides a snapshot of its characteristics in 1941.

Further highlighting the augmentation of the AA of vessels of the class is this photograph of a Kirov-class vessel in the Black Sea in September 1943. In addition to the two 37mm 70-K guns in the foreground and three 100mm B-34 guns behind them, just visible is one of the quad Vickers heavy machine guns added to most vessels of the class. (NH, 100190)

Table 15: Specifications for the cruiser *Petropavlovsk* as of 1941		
Displacement	Normal (tonnes)	10,400
Dimensions	Maximum length (m)	212.5
	Maximum width (m)	21.9
Draught (m)		4.5
Armament	Main	4x203mm (60 cal)
	Anti-aircraft	1 x twin 37mm (83 cal), 9x20mm (65 cal)
Armoured protection	Belt (maximum)/deck (maximum)/bridge (maximum)/main turrets (maximum)	80mm/30mm/150mm/160mm
Crew		232

A wartime midship view of a vessel of the Kirov class showing not only three 100mm B-34 guns but also one set of triple 533mm torpedo tubes. (NH, 95587)

On 17 July 1941, the *Petropavlovsk* was ordered to prepare to serve as a floating battery, with its electrical system and armament readied for operation. Service as a floating battery did not require a full crew, or even that crew already assembled, and many of its existing members were either transferred to other vessels or ended up as part of two companies of infantry that became part of a naval infantry brigade.

After having been towed to a mooring at *Ugol'naia gavan'* from Factory 189 in Leningrad on 14 August 1941, the Soviet naval ensign was raised aboard *Petropavlovsk* the following day. On 7 September, as German forces came within range, its 203mm German-manufactured main guns opened fire on them. Firing daily on advancing German formations, by 17 September it had fired 676 rounds from its main guns. On 11 September, a round exploded in the barrel of one of the guns in the forward turret, meaning that from then on the ship was only firing with three of its main guns.

On 16 September, *Petropavlovsk* suffered its first hit from German artillery fire as enemy forces found their range. Unable to move under its own steam, and even reliant on electrical power from the shore, *Petropavlovsk* had still not been moved by tugs summoned for the purpose before it suffered further hits on 17 September. In the vessel's only partially completed state, its damage-control capabilities were limited, and German artillery kept firefighting tugs from assisting. In the face of such difficulties, the ship was evacuated later that day – having suffered a total of 53 hits from up to 203mm German artillery – and settled on the bottom in the shallow water of its mooring.

With much of its anti-aircraft armament removed, *Petropavlovsk* would continue in this state with only a skeleton crew. Some of those who had been evacuated subsequently participated in a Soviet amphibious operation at Peterhof in early October 1941 that resulted in heavy casualties for little gain, several of the *Petropavlovsk* crew among the many dead.

By September 1942, repairs to *Petropavlovsk* gave it the necessary clearance from the sea floor to allow it to be towed into Leningrad's port. There, its main armament was repaired and it was moved to a firing position within the port, firing a token six rounds that month before falling silent until January 1944. *Petropavlovsk* was then able to offer some support to Soviet offensive operations near Leningrad. On 10 January 1944, it fired 116 rounds at enemy positions as training rounds in support of Soviet offensive operations that began five days later. During five days from 15 January, *Petropavlovsk* fired another 936 rounds, with a further two rounds on 23 January and three on 24 January before its guns ceased firing for good.

Although *Petropavlovsk* was renamed *Tallinn* on 1 September 1944 – at which point there was presumably the intent to finish the ship after the war – it was not completed when hostilities ended, instead serving as an accommodation hulk.

Later examples of Kirov-class cruisers such as *Kalinin* were completed with 85mm 90-K dual-purpose mounts such as this example at the Central Museum of the Armed Forces in Moscow, instead of the 100mm B-34 mounts on earlier vessels. Vessels with this mount were still in service in 1991 when the Soviet Union collapsed. The same mount was used for the 76mm 34-K gun. (AC)

POST-WAR GUN CRUISERS

Although the Soviet Union finished those Project 26-bis vessels that were in advanced states of construction at the beginning of the war during the conflict itself, it also had a number of Project 68 vessels under construction when hostilities broke out. The Project 68 vessels were essentially enlarged and improved Project 26s. While two Project 68 cruisers were scrapped by Germany on the Black Sea, five others were completed as Project 68-K (Chapaev-class) variants after the war. For Stalin, at least, modern gun cruisers still offered the sort of prestige that he apparently craved for his navy, even if during the war they had typically not been employed as intended. Such was the appeal of cruisers that the post-war Sverdlov-class or Project 68-bis vessels were subsequently produced in large numbers – 14 in all.

In addition to having cruisers of Russian or Soviet manufacture in the fleet after the war, the Soviet Union gained the former German light cruiser *Nürnberg* through war reparations. The *Nürnberg* became the *Admiral Makarov* in Soviet service. The Soviet Northern Fleet also operated the US Omaha-class light cruiser *Milwaukee* until 1949, a vessel that had temporarily been provided in 1944 in lieu of reparation vessels and served in the Soviet Northern Fleet as *Murmansk*. In 1949, the Soviet Navy would then receive the Italian light cruiser *Emanuele Filiberto Duca d`Aosta* that was renamed *Stalingrad* before becoming *Kerch'*, serving with the Black Sea Fleet.

CONCLUSION

The relatively modest Soviet pre-war cruiser force arguably played a meaningful local role in the war in the Black Sea from 1941–43, during which time the Soviet Navy was able to use the seaward flank to good effect in a theatre of operations in which the Axis lacked major surface vessels. That this exploitation of the seaward flank was insufficient to change the course of events on land should not detract from the Soviet Navy's contribution to the war in that theatre. In the Baltic, however, the fact that the cruisers were operated for much of the war as glorified gun barges hardly warranted their costs, which was particularly the case for the Project 26 and 26-bis vessels. The fear of losing a major warship that seems to have limited their use is perhaps best indicated by the Soviet Navy's failure to use their cruisers for the interdiction of German maritime communications between the Baltic Republics and the Reich itself during the closing stages of the war.

SELECT BIBLIOGRAPHY

Berezhnoi, S. S. *et al*, *Korabli i vspomogatel'nie suda sovetskogo Voenno-Morskogo Flota (1917–1927 gg.) (Spravochnik)* Voenizdat, Moscow (1981)

Bikov, P. D., 'Perekhod Baltiiskogo flota iz Gel'singforsa v Kronstadt zimoi 1918 g.' in *Morskoi sbornik*, No 11 (1923), pp.13–219

Burov, V. N. and Iukhin, V. E., *Kreiser 'Avrora'. Pamiatnik istorii otechestvennogo korablestroeniia*, Lenizdat, Leningrad (1987)

Chapligin, A., *Kreiser 'Avrora'* Eksmo/Iauza, Moscow (2017)

Chapligin, A., *Kreiser 'Kirov'*, Eksmo/Iauza, Moscow (2017)

Chernishev, A. A., *Gvardeiskie kreisera Stalina – 'Krasnii Kavkaz', 'Krasnii Krim', 'Chervona Ukraina'* Eksmo/Iauza, Moscow (2013)

Chernishev, A. A., 'Kreisera tipa "Kirov"' in *Morskaia Kollektsiia* 1 (49), (2003)

Chernishev, A. A., 'Kreisera tipa "Maksim Gor'kii"' in *Morskaia Kollektsiia* 2 (50), (2003)

Gribovskii, V. Iu., *Morskaia politika SSSR i razvitie flota v predvoennie godi. 1925–1944 gg*, OOO 'Voennaia kniga', Moscow (2006)

Khromov, V. V., 'Kreiser "Oleg"' in *Morskaaia Kollektsiia*, 1 (2006)

Kozlov, S., *Kreiser*, Voenmorizdat, Moscow/Leningrad (1940)

Litvinov, D. V., 'Kreiser "Petropavlovsk" v oborone Leningrada' in *Gangut*, No 45 (2007), pp.86–93

Mel'nikov, P. M., '"Bogatir"' in *Stapel'*, vipusk 6, LeKo, St Petersburg (2009)

Ovsiannikov, S. I., *Istoriia vtorogo rozhdeniia kreisera 'Avrova'*, Izdatel'stvo Gangut, St Petersburg (2020).

Platonov, A. V., *Entsiklopediia sovetskikh nadvodnikh korablei, 1941–1945*, OOO 'Izdatel'stvo Poligon', St Petersburg (2002)

Platonov, A. V., Aprelev, S. V. and Siniaev, D. N., *Sovetskie boevie korabli 1941–1945. IV. Vooruzhenie*, Almanakh 'Tsitadel'', St Petersburg (1997)

Polenev, L. L., *Sto let v spiskakh flota. Kreiser 'Avrora'*, Izdatel'stvo 'Ostrov', St Petersburg (2003)

Skvortsov, A. V., *Gvardeiskii kreiser 'Krasnii Kavkaz'. 1926–1945*, 'Galeia Print', St Petersburg (2005).

Skvortsov, A. V., 'Korabli brigadi kreiserov Chernomorskogo flota v oborone Odessi' in *Gangut*, No 90 (2015), pp.67–88

Skvortsov, A. V., *Kreiser 'Avrora' i ee 'sistershipi' 'Diana' i 'Pallada'*, Eksmo/Iauza, Moscow (2016)

Skvortsov, A. V., 'Kreisera "Krasnii Krim" i "Krasnii Kavkaz" v Kerchensko-Feodosiiskoi desantnoi operatsii' in *Gangut*, No 97 (2017), pp.36–50.

Taras, A. E., *Rossiiskii flot v Velikoi voine 1914–1918 gg*, Kharvest, Minsk (2017)

Tsvetkov, I. F., *Gvardeiskii kreiser 'Krasnii Kavkaz'*, 'Sudostroenie', Leningrad (1990)

Usenko, N. V. *et al* (eds), *Russkii arkhiv: Velikaia Otechestvennaia: Prikazi i direktivi narodnogo komissara VMF v godi Velikoi Otechestvennoi voini. T. 21 (10)*, TERRA, Moscow (1996)

Usov, V. Iu., *Kreiser 'Maksim Gor'kii'*, Izdatel'svto 'Gangut', St Petersburg (1993)

Vasiun'kin, V. V., *Artilleriiskie kreisera VMF SSSR*, 'Morskoe nasledie', St Petersburg (2019)

Zablotskii, V. P., 'Vsiia bogatirskaia rat' (Bronepalubnie kreisera tipa "Bogatir"')', Chast' 1, *Morskaia Kollektsiia* (dopolnitel'nie vipuski), 3 (2010)

Zablotskii, V. P., 'Vsiia bogatirskaia rat' (Bronepalubnie kreisera tipa "Bogatir"')', Chast' 2, *Morskaia Kollektsiia* (dopolnitel'nie vipuski), 1 (2011)

Zuev, G. I., 'Minnii zagraditel' "Marti"' in *Midel'-shpangout*, 14 (2008)

INDEX

Note: Page locators in bold refer to captions, plates and pictures.